"Agi's techniques to bring to life your key messages are thoughtful, creative and above all, very powerful. Her effective use of video (and numerous rehearsals!) resulted in a far better final product, a clear and concise message and a better experience for the audience. She's the consummate professional."

Don Forgeron // President and CEO, Insurance Bureau of Canada

"Agota and her team helped me prepare for media interviews and presentations at some key moments while my organization was undergoing significant change management. Their advice prepared me for a series of interviews, and provided me with practical ideas I was able to apply right away to help me better convey the key messages we were to communicate to our audience. Media relations is an increasingly complicated field, and working through mock interviews including video feedback with The Gabor Group definitely helped my team gain a sense of control and confidence with the process."

Peter Balasubramanian // President and CEO, Tarion

"Tell the truth. Keep it simple. Know your speech and rehearse it. These are just a few of the valuable lessons learned from my coaching and training with The Gabor Group. Like many business sectors, the property and casualty insurance industry is rife with acronyms and industry-specific terms. As an industry spokesperson it is sometimes difficult to break out of the language used within the industry when speaking to other audiences. To this day I remember Agi Gabor advising me "Explain it like you would to Aunt Martha". (The fact that I actually had an Aunt Martha made it even more real and useful!) And while it's necessary to be prepared for the occasional aggressive media interview, the more realistic view from Gabor is that most reporters just want to get at the truth of a story so give it to them. Like the majority of people, public speaking did not come naturally to me but knowing the material and rehearsing it with Gabor certainly reduced anxiety and improved performance comfort. Working with The Gabor Group was a joy and assisted me greatly in my career."

Stan Griffin // Former President and CEO,
Insurance Bureau of Canada

'Efficiency, creativity and professionalism come to mind when I think of the Gabor Group. From concept development to post-production, Agota Gabor and her skilled team have created video content for our events that connects and resonates with the audience and makes our events pop. Innovation and storytelling in one fell swoop."

Tina Kremmidas // Managing Director,
Investment Industry Association of Canada

"Agi brings her wealth of communications knowledge and media experience to the Gabor Group's effective media workshops. She put our team through our paces and we left feeling well equipped to deal with potential questions from the media."

Clare Richardson // Nickel Institute (Brussels, Belgium)

"Agi's presentation and media coaching are second to none. She can help the most senior executive or someone new to an organization improve the skills necessary to make effective and convincing presentations and media interviews."

Nancy Tibbo // Communications Professional

Agota Gabor – Agota is CEO and Founder of The Gabor Group, a Canadian communications agency specializing in Presentation, Public Speaking and Interview Skills Training.

Before founding the company in 1981, Gabor had a successful career in television journalism. She was researcher, reporter, host and producer for the Canadian Broadcasting Corporation in Canada, Europe and the Far East.

She worked for television news as well as various current affairs programs including CBC's *Take 30* and *As it Happens*.

After 10 years and conducting hundreds of television and radio interviews, Gabor saw the need for a service that enables corporate executives, politicians and members of the public to better communicate.

The Gabor Group was the first Canadian company to offer Media Training as a key service and the company still features its now well-known communications skill training workshops and seminars.

General Motors, Coca-Cola, The Bank of Montreal, TD Canada Trust, Insurance Bureau of Canada, OMVIC, Tarion: all have been, and are, some of Gabor's clients, as well as hundreds of staff and management of various Ontario Government Ministries.

Gabor's staff is made up of a diverse group of communications professionals, and as well as communications training, the company now also offers Media Relations, Video Production and Digital Marketing services.

Public Speaking Presentations Media Interviews

Helping you Succeed

AGOTA GABOR

Contents

Public Speaking · Presentations · Media Interviews · Helping you Succeed

www.gaborgroup.com

Cover illustration by Matthew Spence
Book design by Scott McMann
Typefaces: PT Sans and PT Serif

For Bill, Kathy, Carter and Alexis

Foreword

Any student of Agota Gabor soon learns that having a message to communicate—*a story to tell*—is just the first step to being heard, understood, and believed. As she so ably outlines in the pages that follow, there is much to know about effective communications. In *Public Speaking · Presentations · Media Interviews* this veteran trainer provides the toolkit.

For more than twenty years I was a client of The Gabor Group and during that time, I watched Agota transform shy and nervous speakers into effective communicators. Amateur and professional speakers, alike, took the podium with confidence thanks to her coaching sessions.

Agota understands targeted audiences and the best ways to reach them. From wearing the right tie to delivering the right message, she knows it all.

And now, you can too. It's all here in an easily navigated text that encapsulates what you need to know in our sometimes complicated world of communication. Enjoy...

Mary Lou O'Reilly // Former Executive Vice President,
Insurance Bureau of Canada

Introduction

Public Speaking is a performance. We are all nervous before giving a performance and we should be. Nerves give us energy, which we need to perform well.

I am sure Lady Gaga had little butterfly flutters as she walked up to the mic to start singing the American National Anthem at President Biden's inauguration. If she didn't, she couldn't have given that magnificent performance.

Actors will tell you that they need to be a little nervous before going on stage, and Broadway performers are often quoted saying that when playing the same part every night for many months, sometimes years, the butterflies stop fluttering, their excitement and energy level drop and the show starts to look and sound tired.

But let's not confuse a little nervous energy with fear.

Did you ever hear anyone say?

"I fear public speaking more than death"

"I would rather die than speak in front of an audience"

"I don't like to ask questions in front of people"

"If I have to speak in public I have a panic attack"

"What if I forget what I was saying? I would rather not try"

Over the course of 35 years teaching presentation skills and public speaking, I heard some of the above-noted comments from CEOs, politicians, students, job seekers and others. They believed them and stayed away from making speeches, delegating important presentations to juniors. When in public, they kept their opinions to themselves, and never lived up to their own potential.

It has saddened me, because I know it doesn't have to be that way. A little flutter in the tummy is a good thing; we need that nervous energy to perform.

But naturals are made as well as born and there are techniques you can learn that turn *fear into energy* and *speech into communication*!

This book will help you get there.

MEDIA INTERVIEWS

The second half of the book deals with media interviews and how to become an effective spokesperson when representing your company, your brand or yourself.

The skills you will learn will prove useful whether you will be giving different types of media interviews or you want to be effective in your social media, or even when you talk about your job or your hobbies at a backyard BBQ.

Long before I started my business, I was a reporter with CBC TV, when I was assigned to interview a well-known accountant about changes to our tax laws. In our pre-interview he was great at explaining the changes and what they would mean to Canadians.

But when we turned the cameras on, he gave me stiff, technical and complicated answers. Back at the station I edited the story and ended up using a very short clip of him talking, having to do more voice-over narration to explain the tax changes in simple terms.

He called the next day and asked me why I only used a short clip. I explained that my audience wouldn't have understood his complicated answers.

My accountant guest understood and asked me to give him a few lessons on how to give better interviews. He suggested I start a business offering the service.

I only took his advice some ten years later, when I started The Gabor Group. Since then I have had the opportunity to train hundreds of executives, politicians, and people in all areas of life. They, and I, both enjoyed the experience.

I hope you will enjoy both sections of this book and put the tips to use throughout your career and life.

Part 1

Public Speaking and Presentations

Chapter 1

Preparing Your Presentation

AUDIENCE REACTION SCORE

From the moment you enter the room for a job interview, walk up to a podium, or stand up at the dinner table to give a toast, your audience takes your measure. We all react first to the messenger, **then** to the message. First impressions matter and what your audience thinks of you matters. How the audience reacts to you will enhance or undermine your message.

Whenever you speak, you aim to *persuade*.

In a conversation you want to have your opinion *heard* and *agreed* with.

When applying for a job, you want to persuade the interviewer that you are *the one* she should hire.

When giving a toast, you want people to like it. And, when you are giving a speech, you must have an *objective*.

In order to persuade your audience, you should strive for:

CREDIBILITY

LIKEABILITY

MESSAGE

If your audience finds you credible, your chances of persuading them are 40%.

If they actually like you as a speaker, you have another 40% chance to succeed. Understanding and agreeing with the message only counts for 20% in your overall success. Interesting.

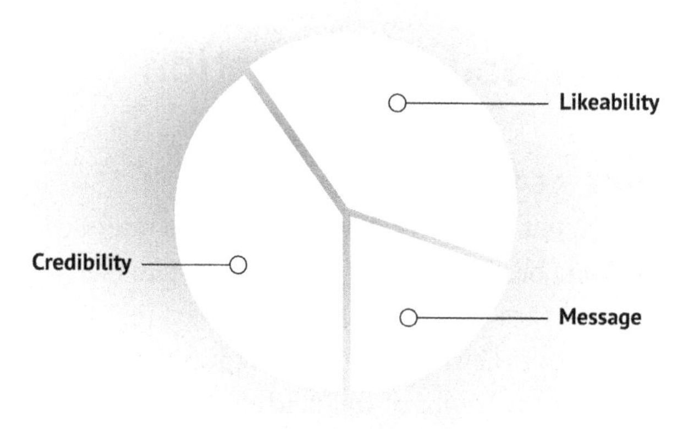

Keep in mind that in order to speak with *confidence* and *style* you must have a *well-written* and *well-prepared* message.

If your points are well prepared, well written and well rehearsed, your message will give you the confidence to be credible and likeable and you will deliver it with an audience reaction score of 100%.

DEVELOPING THE CONTENT

THE RIGHT OBJECTIVE

Determine your needs:

You must be clear about what you want to happen
—and with the results.

Determine your audience's needs:

They need to get something out of your presentation
—to be informed, persuaded or entertained.

An effective presentation is a balance between the speaker's needs and the needs of the audience. Overlapping needs must be met. Every time you speak, you are negotiating, presenting and informing.

The really complete speaker (the "natural") deals with both style and content, and excels at both.

Naturals are made, as well as born.

Before planning the first word of your speech you must systematically assess:

Who, what, why, when, where and how.

TEST YOUR OBJECTIVE

This means examining both your own and your audience's attitudes and knowledge about the subject at hand.

For example:

- Is your audience aware of your subject matter? Do they know anything about it, or are they misinformed?
- Do they have some subjective feelings about your subject matter?

An honest assessment of the attitude of your audience helps you choose a realistic objective.

REACH YOUR OBJECTIVES

KNOW WHAT YOU WANT TO HAPPEN

Make sure you are clear about your goal. How do you want your audience to react to your speech?

CLARIFY YOUR KEY MESSAGE

There may be several messages you wish to get across in your speech, but there must be one that is key—the message that is most important for you to get across.

Deliver your speech/presentation in such way that the audience will get the key message:

- Be clear about your goal
- Don't be too ambitious
- Limit your objectives and limit the data
- Don't neglect rapport and emotional appeals
- Identify the audience's needs and concerns
- Keep it in simple language, structure and format
- Edit out unnecessary points, words or data
- Then edit again

Chapter 2

Structure

In order to get your ideas across to your audience you have to focus your content and present it in a simple, direct, and easy-to-understand and easy-to-remember style.

Memo writing is out. The basic principles of news writing are the rule:

The lead... the core statement

The body... the story itself with macro examples

The summary... re-focusing of the core statement

THE THREE TELLS

The easiest way to understand this concept is through the *three tells* method.

1. **Tell them what you're going to tell them**—signpost, tell them up front the main points and what they can expect from your presentation.
2. **Tell them the heart of your presentation**—these are the statements that say in a few words what you will expand upon and support in your remarks. Give units of information, offer simple illustrations, case histories, and human-scale examples to demonstrate your key points.

3. **Tell them what you've told them**—review what you've covered, distill it to the key points, spell out the logical conclusion and invite action, decision, commitment or challenge.

The *three tells* apply to any kind of speech, long or short, formal or informal.

An example of a formal speech may be the Governor General's Throne speech in 2020. It is a long speech, but its structure is based on the *three tells.*

Here are excerpts from her speech with notes pointing out how the *three tells* are used.

First Tell:

A Stronger and More Resilient Canada

As her first "Tell them what you are going to tell them", she tells us that the pandemic occurred and is real — and she will be talking about its effects and how the government will help.

> *"This pandemic is the most serious public health crisis Canada has ever faced. Over 9,000 Canadians have died in six months. For our neighbours in the United States, this figure is over 200,000. Globally, it's nearly a million. But these aren't just numbers. These are friends and family. Neighbours and colleagues.*
>
> *The pandemic is the story of parents who have died alone, without loved ones to hold their hand. It is the story of kids who have gone months without seeing friends. Of workers who have..."*

Second Tell:

Here, she is telling us how the government is helping:

> *"The first foundation of the Government's approach is protecting Canadians from COVID-19. This is priority number one.*
>
> *It is the job of the federal government to look out for all Canadians and especially our most vulnerable. We need to work together. Beating this virus is a Team Canada effort.*
>
> *Over the last six months, Canadians have stood united and strong. Their actions embody what has always been the purpose of the federal government: bringing*
>
> *Canadians together to achieve common goals.*
>
> *Personal protective equipment has been shipped across the country. Members of the Canadian Forces were there in long-term care homes. Close to 9 million.*
>
> *Canadians were helped with the Canada Emergency Response Benefit and over 3.5 million jobs were supported by the wage subsidy. The Government will continue to have people's backs just like Canadians have each other's backs."*

Third Tell: "Telling them what you told them"

She tells us that the pandemic happened, that the government is helping Canadians and how the government will make things better.

> *"The economic impact of COVID-19 on Canadians has already been worse than the 2008 financial crisis. These consequences will not be short-lived. This is not the time for austerity.*

Canada entered this crisis in the best fiscal position of its peers. And the Government is using that fiscal firepower, on things like the Canada Emergency Response Benefit and the Canada Emergency Wage Subsidy, so that Canadians, businesses, and our entire economy have the support needed to weather the storm. Canadians should not have to choose between health and their job, just like Canadians should not have to take on debt that their government can better shoulder.

As we fight for every Canadian and defend everyone's ability to succeed, we also need to focus on the future, and on building back better. This forms the third foundation of the Government's approach.

Around the world, advanced economies are realizing that things should not go back to business as usual. COVID-19 has exposed the vulnerabilities in our societies.

The Government will create a resiliency agenda for the middle class and people working hard to join it. This will include addressing the gaps in our social systems, investing in health care, and creating jobs. It will also include fighting climate change, and maintaining a commitment to fiscal sustainability and economic growth as the foundation of a strong and vibrant society."

Chapter 3

Choosing your Delivery Style

Some presenters prefer delivering from **fixed text** while others prefer **point form**. Both styles have their advantages and you should choose the one with which you are most comfortable.

But never, **ever** make a speech or presentation *without notes*, no matter how familiar you are with the topic. Prepare, have notes, rehearse, if time permits.

Don't speak "off-the-cuff."

The type of occasion and the size of the audience as well as the physical set-up will also influence your choice of presentation format.

FIXED TEXT

Write your speech in a style that's easy to "lift off" the page.

Write it for the spoken word, not the written one. Write as if for a television newscast, not for the editorial page of *The Globe and Mail* or *The New York Times*.

Short sentences are most important. Active verbs will give your speech more energy.

Text should be formatted for easy reading: using large font and triple-spaced with large margins, not more than three paragraphs on a page. As well, paragraphs should never carry over from one page to another.

Every four pages or so, a paragraph should be designated as an **ad lib**. It should have a code to remind the presenter that the ad lib portion of the speech should be delivered at this point.

Words to be given special emphasis should be underlined. They should be underlined by the presenter (**not** the speech writer, if there is one) during the rehearsal of the presentation.

Presentations should always be rehearsed out loud. Silent reading does not help much with delivery.

SAMPLE SPEECH MARKED UP FOR DELIVERY:

It is important to mark up your speech for delivery. Here are some markings you can use:

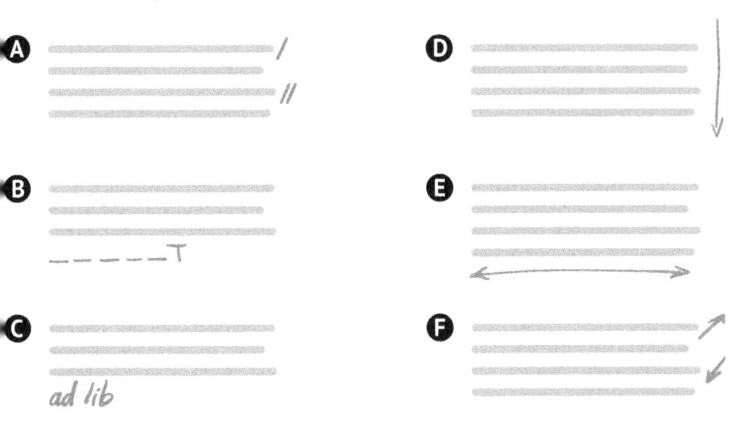

SLASHES

A – Slashes mark the pauses.

TRANSITIONS

B – Marks a new thought or Transition.

STORY

C – Ad Lib – generally should be about a personal experience.

D – Line with a downward arrow on the side means speak faster, not too dramatic.

E – Line with arrows on both sides means slow down.

F – Short arrows pointing diagonally up or down are markers for your inflection to go up—or down—at the end of the sentence.

Here are excerpts from a speech I marked up for the President of The Insurance Bureau of Canada, Don Forgeron. He gave this speech to the annual NICC (National Insurance Conference of Canada).

The Opening

////

Good Afternoon.

////

When I was growing up, / we all knew the big technology companies: / IBM, / Xerox / and the like. / They were big corporations, / some of the largest on the face of the earth. //

Yet so much of what they did seemed distant, / mysterious, / almost magical. /// It's not like it is with smart phones / – we wouldn't exactly come home from school / and spend hours alone in our bedrooms / staring at a photocopier. //

Technology was important, / but largely removed from our daily lives. //

Today, / every company is a tech company. / You can't operate and succeed in business / without an understanding of technology—and how best to use it / to pursue and achieve your competitive goals. //

The whole economy is the tech sector./ And today,/ every person is in IT. //

We all have to manage our phones, / our tablets / and laptops. /

We all have to reboot our parents' Wi-Fi. //

We all have fingertip access / to all that the world has to offer online. //

_ _ _ _ _T

Think about it this way: / In 1999—less than 20 years ago – humanity was creating 1.5 billion gigabytes of data every year. // In 2016, / we're producing 2.3 trillion gigabytes of data... every day. //

Today, a 3-year-old uses technology in a way / that would astound the computer pioneers of the early 1950s. //

_ _ _ _ _T

[SLIDE: historic photograph of early computer]

UNIVAC was the first "mass-produced" commercial computer. /

It weighed 29,000 pounds, / which made it tricky to bring on board with your carry-on. //

[Don looks up at the slide.]

Not to date myself, / but that's only slightly bigger than my first cell phone. //

Our world has changed, / obviously. /

But what's truly striking today is the pace of change. ///

It took half a century to get from the UNIVAC to the iMac. / ↗
It took a decade / to get from an MP3 player that maxed out at 30 songs / ↗ to a streaming service that makes access to almost every song ever written/ as close as your smart phone. / ↙

Across industries and around the world, / the speed and scope of change is weakening, / undermining and ultimately disrupting the foundation of many traditional businesses. // ↙

The story

We tend to think of disruption as a new concept,/ the kind of idea that might have been invented at a TED talk. //

But let me tell you about Joseph Schumpeter (SHOOM-payter). //
Growing up in Europe,Joseph set himself three goals in life: //

to be the greatest economist on the planet

the best horseman in all of Austria

and the greatest lover in all of Vienna

READING FROM A TELEPROMPTER

The script on the prompter should be marked for pauses and transitions the same way as shown in the sample script for fixed text.

Marking your script is very important. There are various ways to do it and you should use the one most comfortable to you.

There are a few techniques that are effective when reading a prompter.

Look down from the screen between sentences as if you are taking a look at your script. Pretend that the prompter is a person you are talking to. Lead the prompter (read ahead of the text on the screen); don't follow it.

I trained a president of a company who insisted that for every important speech, I should sit somewhere in the audience where he could see me, and I would give him hand signals, directing him to slow down, speed up, hold a pause, etc.

We all develop our own way of prompting ourselves to perform well.

POINT FORM

Write your presentation first as if for fixed text. Rehearse it out loud, to register chosen words to your *audio memory*.

Prepare bullet points from the text, as if you were preparing for a PowerPoint presentation.

Write bullet points on the left side of a double-column script.

If lost for the exact word or phrase, look at your prepared text on the right side of the script.

Statistics or complicated text should be read from a prepared script.

Here is a script example, using the same speech for point form double-column, with points on left and script on right.

Two-column script

Points	Text
	Good Afternoon.//////////
Big companies and big computers	When I was growing up,/ we all knew the big technology companies:/ IBM,/ Xerox/ and the like./ They were big corporations,/ some of the largest on the face of the earth. //
	Technology was important,/ but largely removed from our daily lives.//
Today everyone is in IT	Today,/ every company is a tech company./ You can't operate and succeed in business/ without an understanding of technology – and how best to use it/ to pursue and achieve your competitive goals.//
	The whole economy is the tech sector./ And today,/ every person is in IT.//
	We all have to manage our phones,/ our tablets/ and laptops./
	We all have to reboot our parents' Wi-Fi.//
	We all have fingertip access/ to all that the world has to offer online.//

Chapter 4

Visual Aids

There are many visual aids available, but regardless of which you choose, you must keep in mind that YOU ARE THE PRESENTER. The visual aids are there to help you, but you shouldn't depend on them to tell your story.

Choose the visual aid according to the size and formality of your audience, your budget and your message.

Flip charts and over-heads are now old school and few people use them. Although I must say, a dog trainer offering to teach my dog how not to bark, used a flip chart very effectively.

Most visual aids are now seen on a computer screen or on a tablet in a PowerPoint or Keynote presentation. Whether you use words, illustrations, cartoons, video or multi-media, the key is to keep them simple. Make sure you are comfortable with your aids and the mechanics of them.

It is crucial that your aids don't confuse your audience and that you keep their maximum attention.

Pictures and graphic illustrations are much more effective than words.

If you use words, use only a few.

Don't write a speech for your PowerPoint presentation and then read it off the screen.

KEEP IN MIND: Your aids are there to help you.

BUT

You are the presenter.

Chapter 5

Delivering Your Presentation

DELIVERING YOUR PRESENTATION

The key words are: PREPARATION and REHEARSAL.

You know WHAT to say. Learn HOW to say it.

PREPARE and REHEARSE.

Keep these key points in mind:

AUTHORITY

If you are going to make a presentation or a speech, you should know what you're talking about; you know your subject matter.

You must also look, and act, knowledgeable.

ENERGY

An energetic speaker is absorbed in what he/she is saying and sounds as if he/she cares about the topic. Give as much energy to speaking as you want the audience to give to listening.

If you're not excited about the topic, why should your audience be?

EYE CONTACT

Be aware of the audience. The speaker must be willing to see and respond to the audience, constantly surveying person by person.

Really look into people's eyes. Don't just look above them. Pick out a person to your right, middle and left, and a couple in the back. Don't look at any one person for too long. Move your eyes around.

BODY LANGUAGE

Your body is also making a speech. Make sure it is the same speech!

Stand erect with feet shoulder-width apart. Knees should be slightly bent (this becomes comfortable with practice.) You can move around and change position, if you have a reason to do so.

For example, when you wish to make a point, step and lean forward or step away from the podium, etc. But don't sway, or walk around without a reason. That is a nervous move and the audience will recognize it as such.

Your hands and what to do with them? This is a problem for many presenters. Don't cross them in front of you and don't put them behind your back. These are defensive postures and they will stop you from gesturing.

If it is natural for you to gesture, then gesture. And make your gestures big and meaningful.

Make sure the gestures are well timed.

DEFENSIVE

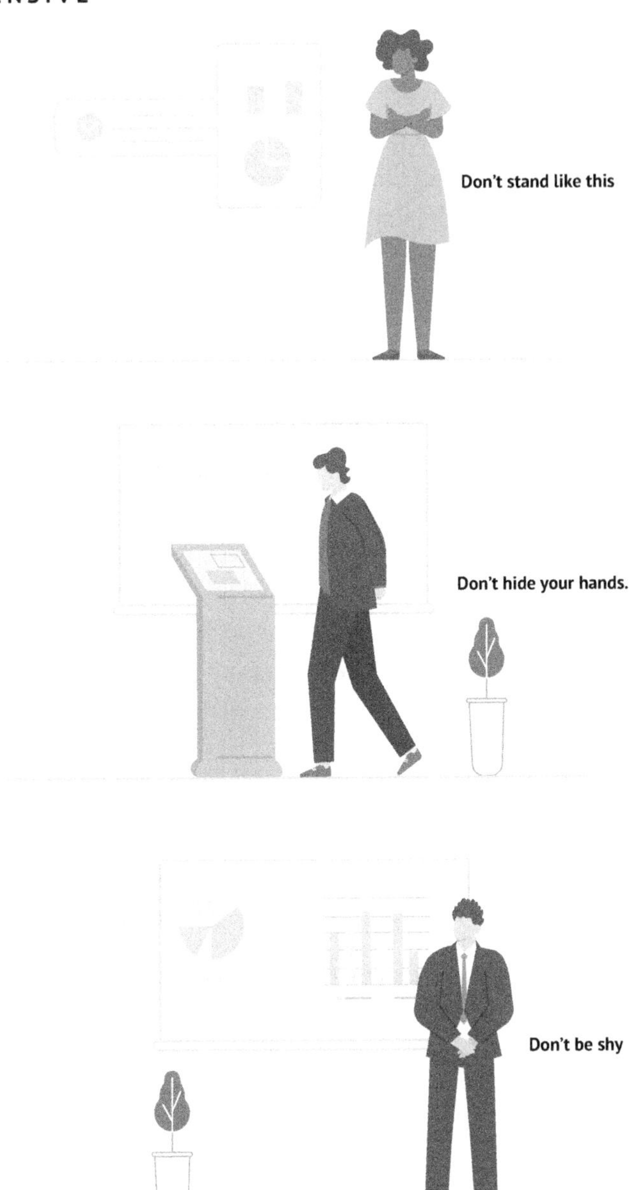

HOW SHOULD YOU STAND?

Stand straight with shoulders back and your arms relaxed at your sides, or bent at the elbows around waist-high, a posture which allows you to gesture.

You can also rest your arms on the podium, but if you do, make sure you do it lightly; don't squeeze the podium as if you were hanging onto it for your life! I have seen some light podiums almost fall over, so be careful.

CAN I PUT MY HANDS IN MY POCKET?

A FREQUENTLY ASKED QUESTION

Depends when, is my answer. You wouldn't want to walk into a meeting with your hands in your pockets and you shouldn't have your hands in your pockets at the beginning of your presentation. When you reach the ad lib, informal part of your speech, you may put a hand in your pocket. Don't leave it in there for long and make sure there is no change or keys in your pockets so you won't be tempted to jiggle them, which would be distracting.

PAUSES AND TRANSITIONS

The audience only hears your speech once. Allow them to understand it.

Give them *time* to digest what you are saying.

Pauses are very important.

Mark your script for pauses. One, two and three beat pauses. Depending on the content, if you want a word to stand out, give a pause before and after delivering it.

Don't be afraid of silence. Spoon-feed the audience by your emphasis and delivery.

Transitions are long pauses enhanced with a body movement.

In most presentations/speeches there are four or five key points to make.

In between those points, there should be a transition.

Mark transitions on your script.

VOICE INFLECTION

When we speak in conversation, we end some of our sentences up and some of them down [raised vs lowered]. This is natural. When we deliver a speech we must also be natural. Many speakers drop the end of all sentences and deliver their speeches in a monotone voice.

Practice this: speak as if you were speaking with someone.

Remember to mark up and down inflections with arrows at the end of your sentences.

ATTENTION LADIES

Because of the still existing gender inequality in management positions, I trained many more men than women during the past 35 years, but many of the women I trained faced a common challenge.

They projected a kind of apology for being at the podium and giving a speech or presentation.

This attitude can show in the way you stand as well as in the way you speak. Women tend to deliver statements as if they were asking questions, ending powerful sentences with the inflection up, as if they had question marks at the end.

Become aware if you are doing that and practice until you don't. Record your speech and listen to it; do it again until the question mark in your voice is gone.

Another important thing to watch for is voice projection. When we women project and put energy and emphasis into our delivery, we can end up sounding shrill. I suggest trying to start an octave lower than your speaking tone, so when you want to emphasize your point with increased energy and volume, your voice will sound natural and convincing.

WHEN ENGLISH IS NOT YOUR NATIVE TONGUE

When we speak, our objective is to communicate, whether we speak with an Oxford English, East Indian, or Hungarian accent. It doesn't matter what accent we have, as long as our audience clearly understands what we are saying.

When I started in this business, foreign accents and foreign-sounding names were not welcome on television, radio or at the podium and non-native speakers had to work extra hard to be heard. Fortunately that has changed.

But the need to clearly communicate will never change.

If English is not your first language and if you have a foreign accent, be aware of it.

The solution is to SLOW down.

You can have the best speech in the world, but if your audience needs to strain to understand you, they will be uncomfortable and lose interest in what you have to say.

THE FIRST MINUTE OF YOUR SPEECH

The first minute is the most difficult part of your speech.

When you first arrive at the podium, take your time. Look at your audience; arrange your papers and your microphone.

Remember, you are not ON until you begin to speak, so take your time, and get comfortable with your space.

Start with something very easy—maybe your name, or "*It's nice to be here.*"

After the first pleasantries, take a long pause and then start into your speech.

Don't forget to breathe; it will help.

Presentation Skills Workshops

The most important things you can do in order to become an effective presenter are to prepare and to practice.

You can do that on your own and you can also take a variety of courses, workshops and seminars. From Toastmasters to private coaches, there are professionals who will be happy to help you.

Each workshop will be different, but I can give you a brief description of what you may expect from a Presentation Skills workshop at the Gabor Group.

We hold our workshops in a large meeting room equipped with video equipment and a playback monitor. For a group of three to five participants you would have one consultant and a camera operator working with you.

After introductions, there is a discussion about each person's experience with public speaking and we also discuss emotions related to it (fear, nerves, fun).

We then ask each person to stand up and tell us about themself, his job, or hobby. This is to **break the ice** and to get them used to speaking to the group.

The group is then asked to make notes or write a short speech about themselves—same subject—in preparation for a little longer (3–4 minutes) presentation, that will be recorded and then played back to the group.

Each person delivers their **speech which is recorded**.

We **play back** each recording and **discuss** each person's performance. We discuss the importance of reading as if you were having a conversation and techniques that allow you to do that.

The next element of the workshop is to work on **the first minute of a presentation**. Most of us find the first minute the hardest.

We practice the speaker's entrance to the room, thanking the person who introduced him, checking the podium, the microphone, making sure everything is perfect, looking at the audience, finding a few friendly faces for eye contact.

Then when it is all done, saying: "*Good Afternoon*" and starting with something very simple, something that you can't possibly forget...like your name, or "*Thanks for inviting me*". Then a long pause, a little change in the way you stand, and then the first paragraph.

We record each participant delivering this very important first minute and play that back to the group for discussion.

*We then have a **working lunch**.*

Next we give participants a short speech and we practice **marking it for delivery**. We mark pauses, transitions, volume, speed, and inflections.

We then start practicing the delivery of a **fixed text** speech.

We split participants into two rooms: in one, the trainer works with one participant, in the other, the rest of the participants practice their delivery.

During the one-on-one workshop we practice all aspects of the delivery, lifting the words off the page; pauses, transitions, body language, eye contact, speed, volume, inflections.

Then we **record the performance**. When all participants have done the one-on-one work and have recorded their speech, we get the group back together and **play back** each performance. We stop the tape often for self-critique and **feedback** from the trainer and the group.

The final part of the workshop is working on delivery skills from **point form**, practicing and recording performances.

We wrap up with a **Q&A** and all participants receive an individual post-workshop report.

Remember, public speaking is an important skill.

It CAN be fun and it CAN be learned.

The key is to:

PREPARE AND REHEARSE

PREPARE AND REHEARSE

PREPARE AND REHEARSE

PREPARE AND REHEARSE

PREPARE AND REHEARSE

Part 2

Media Interviews

Chapter 6

Why would you speak with the Media?

Journalists are storytellers. They want you to tell your story and at times you *want* them to tell your story.

Hundreds of years ago, if you wanted to tell your story you went to the town square and shouted it through a paper cone and later a loudspeaker.

Some years later you could print your story and distribute it through a pamphlet. After that came newspapers, radio, television and the internet. The platforms change but that doesn't really matter. The style in which you tell your story changes but the idea behind it remains the same: telling your story.

If you are a celebrity, a politician or a criminal, the media will come to you and ask you to tell them your story. Sometimes they demand your story and want to know all the details.

If you are a business person, an entrepreneur or an inventor, you need to go to the media and get them interested in your story and tell it to the audiences you want to engage. The media can give authority and credibility to your story.

Working for a business, be it your own or a multinational corporation, if it is your responsibility to speak to the media, you become a *media spokesperson.*

As a media spokesperson you need to understand the media, how it works and how you can best work with them and represent your company in the most positive manner.

Here are some things you could find interesting.

THE MEDIA

WHAT IS NEWS?

Two of the most respected Television newsmen of the 20th century, David Brinkley and Chet Huntley were asked the question: ***What is news?*** Brinkley replied: "*News is the unusual, the unexpected.*" His partner was characteristically blunt. "*News,*" Huntley said, involves the "*warts on society's skin; its aberrations.*"

I wouldn't want to go that far, but it is true that disasters make news stories more often than success stories.

Even the dictionaries come up with only half-hearted attempts. Webster's says news is a "*report of recent events; newsworthy matter.*" For "*newsworthy*" it adds: "*sufficiently interesting to the general public to be worth reporting.*"

News, then, is really what you define it to be. But let me suggest some guidelines as to what makes news:

- Disasters
- Wars
- Political change
- Celebrities

Other factors influencing news worthiness:

- Timeliness
- Proximity of the event
- Prominence of persons
- Significance of the event
- Conflict
- Human interest

News is information, conflict and drama.

News is anything the editors and news directors think matters or affects their readers, listeners, or viewers (very subjective.)

News reporting is a competitive business. The battle for readership or ratings breeds competition between the types of media or between similar media outlets.

Each looks for the news story, angle, piece of information, which also helps a news story stay alive.

This competition is particularly intense in big cities with multiple news outlets. Smaller cities usually have one daily, which also competes with the national media for reader attention. There is similar competition among electronic media.

One observer defines the public's point of view of news as:

> "***Must have,***" i.e. the weather, new taxes, a disaster or threat close to home;
>
> "***Nice to know,***" i.e. traffic, baseball score, a house fire;
>
> "***The passing parade,***" i.e. most 'big' stories that happen 'out there.' It's news as entertainment.

STYLE

Most print journalists develop their stories by placing all the important information – the answers to the five W's: the who, what, where, when and why – at the beginning of the story. This ensures that the key facts of the story will appear should the publications' editor have to cut the copy in the interest of space.

This may explain why much of the interview you have given does not appear.

When interviewed, ensure you know the answers to the five W's in advance.

BE AWARE

Television, and radio stations, news websites such as the *Huffington Post* have roving camera persons in the community, capturing events that often appear on newscasts. When in the community, staff should be aware of this possibility and act accordingly.

With social media influencers and phone photographers everywhere, citizen reporters are becoming an important source of news. Be aware of the credibility of sources and try to double-check the source to make sure you are not being served up Fake News.

Chapter 7

The Media and Their Platforms

PRINT

DAILIES

Compared to television and radio, which put severe time constraints on the length of news stories, the daily newspapers, because of space, have the option to cover events in more detail.

They take the time to inform the reader and explain in more detail what's going on. Interviews for print are most likely to be done over the phone, or even via email. Time is of no essence, but preparation is still important. It is easy to be misquoted in a long, rambling interview.

Think out and write your notes, so you know what your agenda is for your interview. Find out who is going to conduct the interview and if possible, read some of his or her previous reports.

WEEKLIES

Due to the competition from online platforms and budget cuts in the industry, the number of weeklies are in decline. It is too bad, because contrary to popular misconceptions, weekly or community newspapers are well read in communities, primarily because they provide information of a local nature.

Their focus is often less "newsy" and immediate, in that the story probably has broken already on newscasts and in the dailies.

Their deadlines tend to be less strict than the dailies, which allows them to take the time to investigate.

Weeklies are ideal to promote your local business. Try to come up with a good local hook for your story and you will be amazed how much publicity they give you.

There are services today that will take your story and distribute it to all weekly papers across the country. It is a worthwhile exercise.

MAGAZINES

Reporters for magazines develop feature stories and provide in-depth coverage of the story, which often involves investigation of the facts behind the headlines. *Rolling Stone*, *The New Yorker*, *Maclean's* and *Time* magazines are examples.

You need to have a pretty big story or a very interesting angle to interest magazines. Remember they have long lead times, sometimes up to three months, so make sure your story is not time sensitive.

RADIO

NEWS

Radio informs rather than explains the news and other than the internet, it is the quickest way to get information to the public. Radio, like online news is 24 hours a day.

Most radio news stories are less than 30 seconds. This makes it important for you as a spokesperson to get the message delivered in the most concise way possible. This will avoid excessive editing of your comments or a decision by the reporter not to run your comments at all.

News items usually have a six-hour life unless new information becomes available.

PUBLIC AFFAIRS

These shows are primarily on national networks such as CBC, PBS and educational stations, although some private radio stations have them. Local morning shows are examples. Their objective is usually to look behind the news story to elaborate and generate controversy if possible and if appropriate.

Occasionally, statements made during these interviews are used later in the form of a news item on the subject.

TELEVISION

NEWS

Informs with strong visual impact.

According to one industry observer, TV is 7% words, 40% voice and 53% nonverbal. How you appear on television is as important as what you say.

TV reporters are looking for a 15–30 second clip, so give your information concisely.

Remember that in addition to the supper and late-night newscasts, some stations carry morning and noon hour newscasts. So give a short and longer clip, to give the editors a choice.

PUBLIC AFFAIRS

Examples include shows such as *60 Minutes*, *The Fifth Estate* and *W5*. Their style is highly investigative.

Consider an invitation to participate carefully because the show often has a preconceived agenda and the format allows for heavy editing. This could result in your comments being taken out of context.

If invited by the above programs, you should immediately involve your Public Affairs or Communications department.

DIGITAL

Most traditional news outlets, print, radio and TV have their news in digital format on their websites.

There are also many online only sources, with podcasts and blogs.

The turnaround time for your information is almost instant. Digital is current and constantly updated.

As to the interview style, similar rules as in print apply.

SOCIAL MEDIA

Short text often accompanied by still or animated photos and short videos.

Social media communications take place on a variety of platforms: Facebook, Instagram, Twitter, SnapChat, YouTube, TikTok and more.

Anything communicated on these platforms is called CONTENT, which tells a mini story. Effective visuals are very important.

BLOGS, VLOGS AND PODCASTS.

Blogs and Vlogs are the internet versions of often subjective print essays with pictures, video and audio. They are popular and an innovative way to get your opinion and messages out.

Podcasts are digital radio documentaries. Storytelling at its best.

IMPORTANT TO REMEMBER

The platform doesn't change the importance of having a strong message that is well prepared and well rehearsed.

Whether you communicate on twitter, give an interview on a podcast, post a video on Facebook or Instagram, the same basic rules of communications apply.

Have a clear objective. Know your audience. Know what result you want.

In today's world you need to be aware how fast content -an interview clip, a comment or a picture — travels from platform to platform. A comment you make in a YouTube video can easily be lifted and presented in a different context on twitter.

Be aware of what you put out there...anywhere, it can both help you or harm you.

ROLES AND AGENDA OF MEDIA PERSONNEL

EDITORS / NEWS DIRECTORS / ASSIGNMENT EDITORS

It is their job to assign reporters to cover stories and decide what potential or ongoing issues matter most. They usually edit the stories that are submitted.

Editors also traditionally follow the editorial position or point of view determined by the publisher or station manager.

Their agenda is to "get the story."

If you are sending out a news release, send it to the Assignment Editor.

REPORTERS AND THEIR AGENDA

In developing a working relationship with reporters, it is important to understand the media from their perspective.

It is their job to research and report or write the news story.

It's a highly competitive business and has a career path that is built on high profile.

Many reporters are generalists who cover a wide variety of subjects, therefore it is wise to assume that they know little about the story at hand and it is your job to ensure that they understand what you have to say.

They're often in a rush, can be under stress, and can be assertive.

They want to get the key facts.

Most reporters try to be fair, yet sometimes get things wrong. If that happens, if you are misquoted, don't get mad. Try to fix it for the next time. Try to contact the reporter, perhaps invite her for coffee and explain your business. Reporters are curious and it is in their interest to learn about various businesses and industries.

Chapter 8

What to do When Reporters Call

DON'T SHOOT FROM THE HIP!

This section focuses on tips and techniques on how to prepare and answer both routine and tough media questions or what to do when the media calls in non-crisis situations.

ASK QUESTIONS

If you or your company is currently involved in a newsworthy issue, or if you are doing a publicity outreach, and the phone rings and you see that it is a reporter, make sure you first ask your questions before giving your answer. "*What did you say your name is? From which publication or station? What subject, and what particular aspect interests you?*" (By understanding the context, and how the question fits into that story, you can avoid giving unnecessary information.)

What is your deadline? If time permits or is needed, it is better to call the reporter back with the full and correct facts, but it is important to get back to the reporter when promised, even if you do not have the answer.

NEGOTIATE

Remember that you can control several key points:

- Make sure you will have time to prepare yourself;
- Try to pick a location in which you are comfortable—on site or in your office;
- Discuss the subject area the interview will cover (and how much or how little to say.)

Chapter 9

The Interview as an Opportunity: How to Make it Work For You

OBJECTIVE

Your objective is to get your or your company's message across. Remember, you are on air to further your company's image or cause. You are not there to be a movie star. Make your points and you will end up with minutes of very valuable commercial air time.

REACHING YOUR OBJECTIVE

1. **DECIDE** how you can best use the opportunity.
2. **WHAT** do you want to tell the world? (Not too ambitious.) Three key messages.
3. **WRITE** a statement in twelve simple words or less.
4. **PREPARATION is the KEY**. Know your strengths and your vulnerabilities.
5. **ORGANIZE** your agenda.
6. **TELL** your tale to somebody you know (not a colleague.) Imagine that person is listening. Keep the language simple; avoid jargon.

7. **DON'T** win a debate on points. Win the listener as a friend.
8. **MAINTAIN** your control of the interview.
9. **GOOD** posture makes for vitality in the interview and voice.
10. **WELCOME** the phone-in opportunity as a chance to be the consumer's friend.

Chapter 10

Some basics

In any type of interview situation both the interviewer and the interviewee should have an agenda.

The journalist wants to find out about you, your brand, your book, or your idea. She represents not just herself but also her audience. She knows her audience and their interests.

She will control the interview and make sure that the conversation doesn't get boring, and won't make her audience stop reading or switch the channel.

You should also have an agenda. I suggest you have three points you want to get across during a 5 to 7 minute long interview. You are not there just to give answers. An interview is a conversation and you have every right to ask a question or change the subject.

Or, think of it as a tennis match in which **you have every right to serve**.

The interviewer and you should respect each other's goals. She invited you to talk about Book A, and let's say your goal is to talk about Book B. You have to respect her goal and she will respect yours.

So you talk a little about Book A, and then switch the topic - BRIDGE to the subject and talk about Book B.

Learning to bridge is important. However, if you totally ignore the question you will alienate your audience and your interviewer.

Example: the 2020 US Debate between former VP Mike Pence and former Senator Kamala Harris

THE DIFFERENT TYPES OF INTERVIEWS

THE CONVERSATIONAL INTERVIEW

Think of morning shows. They should resemble a conversation. During this style of interview, it is quite easy to get your agenda across. Most of the time, the host will prompt you to tell your story. Try to make your points early on in the interview. Here is an interview sample.

This transcript is from the CTV Television program "*The Marilyn Denis Show*". Marilyn (MD) is interviewing the great Canadian opera singer, Measha Brueggergosman (MB) and Dr. Sharon R. (Dr. R) The interview is about Measha's two open-heart surgeries:

> **MD:** How young were you when you had your first episode?
>
> **MB:** Oh I was in my late 20s and I knew that I had a history of cardiac issues in my family and I had my aortic dissection in my early 30s. And then the second one happens almost 10 years later.
>
> **MD:** Is that... part 2, that story, I want to emphasize before we talk to some people who have written to us, how early some of these things show up. Sometimes we don't know when we are younger that we have inherited something but these are not new statistics.

DR. R: It's true and we know we've made huge advances and Measha and I were talking about it earlier, there has never been a better time to be a woman.

Cardio vascularity and death from heart attack is going down, but the group we are seeing, which is concerning, is young women. And how we can get that message out to women to listen to their bodies and know the risks that they have.

MD: Okay. I want to share some stories we received from viewers after last year's show. They could help someone watching TODAY. Lyann wrote: I went to the doctor with a few concerns and was sent home with allergy meds. It didn't sit right with me, so I went that same day to another doctor. A few weeks later I had to have two stents put in.

Ladies, trust yourself and get answers.

MB: That's exactly what happened to me. I felt something. The paramedics came. I went to a hospital. My blood pressure was like 220 over 160 or something insane. They lowered it and regulated it and scheduled me for an MRI later in the week and I would have been long since dead.

But I woke up the next morning and I was like: something is NOT right and I went to my GP and all hail the GP. Your family doctor keeps your records and he thought I was having an embolism because of all the travel as he knew how much I travel. He knew my life.

He knew the stress levels and he sent me right down to Toronto General and that's where the technician gasped [laughs] and I was like: Your poker face is the WORST!

INVESTIGATIVE INTERVIEW

When a reporter is investigating a specific story, i.e., extremely high profits during the pandemic, we call this an "investigative" story. You need to have your facts ready to go. If you don't, tell the interviewer you don't have enough information to do the interview, or, that you are not the right person to speak to her about the subject and give her the name of someone you think she should speak with.

ANTAGONISTIC INTERVIEW

Some interviewers have a reputation to be tough, go for blood. "*So how big was the knife you used to kill your wife?*" Sometimes it is best not to appear on that type of show unless you have to. If you do, don't fight, but try to get your story out, or just repeat that you don't agree and ask the reporter to let you have your say.

A seasoned interviewee can control these situations. It is not easy.

Here is an example from 1983, from CBC's "*The Journal*", a national prime-time Public Affairs program. The interview was conducted by host Barbara Frum (BF), with British Prime Minister Margaret Thatcher (MT).

Note how Mrs. Thatcher takes control of the interview.

> **BF:** ... there is a message that you hate softness. You hate slackers, don't you?
>
> **MT:** Hate? No. It's not a question of hating it. I know that we're only going to get the kind of country and the kind of prosperity, and the kind of standard which I wish to see, if everyone says: it's MY job to do MY best. It's MY job to try to lend a hand to others. And NOT to say: Well, I'm not going to

do that; that's for the state. What sort of society do you think we'd have if you had people saying it's the state's job to find a job? It's the state's job to house me.

It's the state's job to look after my family.

Once you go – freedom is inseparable from personal responsibility. The famous quote from George Bernard Shaw if I can remember it: "*Freedom incurs responsibility. That's why many men fear it.*"

BF: Mrs. Thatcher, what about the losers in this recession? The Canadians who have no jobs or 3 million Britons who have no jobs. EVERY forecaster says we will not return, even with recovery, to the employment patterns of the past. Our politicians also talk, as you do, about high tech jobs, about micro-technology. Not everyone who used to work as a steelworker is going to be in the high-tech industry.

MT: I quite agree he isn't. There are enormous expanses for example in the services industries. But the question you SHOULD be asking, with respect, and every commentator should be asking, AND answering, is: where are the new jobs going to come from? But it's not that difficult. You've only to look back at past experience to see where they DO come from. They come from the creation of wealth by small business starting and growing into big and HOW do you start up a business? By spotting a need, a gap which hasn't been filled.

It may be a service which people WANT and be prepared to pay for, which is not being provided. It may be a new design of textiles...

BF: [inaudible]

MT: No. No. No. The point is this. That is done by men and women of talent, inventive genius, who build businesses and who just have got a way with the market place. It isn't done by the pontification either by a politician [pointing back to herself] or by commentators [pointing to BF].

Now, it is MY politics that in the end this is going to create far more jobs because we are freeing things up for those who have that talent and ability, who are entrepreneurs, to be able to exercise it...

BF: ... I want to ask you so many things. I want to hear what you think about public works but I know we are under a time pressure and I'm going to not ask you about public works. But what about ...

MT: Well do! No you can't just raise it and then leave it. We have a certain amount of public works and I'd like to do more capital work, but what I have to think of is the total public expenditure, the total burden that we put on the taxpayer, and the taxpayer individual men and women, and companies. I have to think of the total burden WITHIN that total burden...

But so often, people say no, I want BIGGER pay in the public sector and I say to them: if you take out bigger pay, I haven't got enough money for new roads or new equipment or new scientific equipment or some of the research institutions. You MUST face people up with choices. Life is made up with choices. And you've got to make responsible choices.

That's what democracy is all about.

NEWS CLIP

In this situation, the question is not heard and the reporter is not seen. A voice over narration introduces the subject and then your comment/clip is edited in. Ideally, it should be 20 seconds or less, but certainly not over 30 seconds.

You cannot bridge in this situation, because your clip won't be used.

Don't say *no comment.* If you don't want to answer a question, say I am sorry, I can't answer that. If you do answer, keep it concise and short. If you make a mistake, you can say, let me start again and do it again.

Reporters like that, as they don't have to do the editing.

Chapter 11

Interview Tips

Before the interview most likely you will be sitting in the green" room, a space near the studio where the interview will take place. The host or the producer will want to chit-chat. You may or may not be comfortable with chatting.

It is all right to say you want to think about the interview.

Don't rehearse your points with the host, you may end up, later in the actual interview, saying "*As I told you earlier...*" Thinking about your points is a better idea.

How you sit is important. Crossing your legs works for most people. Don't swivel as it is very distracting. If they give you a swivel chair, you should try and get another one. Remember that you are on camera during the entire interview. Don't smile or nod if the interviewer is saying something you don't agree with.

Start the interview with "*Thank you for having me*".

If you don't understand a question, ask the host to clarify. You can also paraphrase the question and perhaps even change it to one that you would prefer to answer.

If you really want to say something, lean forward, use your body language to express that you wish to speak, but don't touch the host.

Don't be combative. You can't win, and remember, the audience likes the host; they don't want you to make her look bad.

Learn to bridge from subject to subject, but be subtle.

No Comment is a no-no.

If you don't want to or can't answer a question, say so and say why.

"*I really don't know the answer to that*" or "*I wish I could answer you, but it is not for me to do so.*"

CRISIS SITUATIONS

Every organization big or small, should have a Crisis Management Plan. And an important part of that plan should deal with reaction to the media.

This plan should be detailed in all aspects.

For example: who are the persons designated to speak to the media in case of crisis situations? List every possible crisis that could occur, from fraud, to fire to the departure of a key employee.

Develop template messages which can quickly be adapted to specific situations.

Telling the truth and being transparent is most important in any type of crisis situation. Remember how many times you heard the expression: *the cover-up is worse than the lie.*

Style wise, handle the crisis situation, as you would handle a news clip. If you have the facts, keep your answers short and concise. If you don't have the answer, say so in a polite way. Don't say: "*no comment*" but you can say: "*I am sorry, I don't have the answer*", or "*I am sorry I can't answer that question at this time*".

Chapter 12

Appearance

WHAT TO WEAR

TELEVISION INTERVIEWS OR PUBLIC SPEAKING ENGAGEMENTS

Your appearance communicates your image. How we look influences the way others perceive us and how they react to us.

Most people don't like to admit their judgement of others is based on such superficial data; but being human, those who appeal to our senses tend to attract and influence us disproportionately.

How we present ourselves says something about us. Therefore, our presentation begins with how we dress.

For men, suits are always appropriate, but these days a smart shirt and jacket is also fine. Pastel colours in a business suit are a welcome change. A brightly-coloured tie should complement dark suits.

However, avoid wearing ties with checkered patterns. Shirts, preferably blue, are also flattering for television appearances.

Striped shirts with striped ties are fine, but make sure that the stripes are not all the same width or colour. Sometimes two different stripes can look very natural and attractive. Stripes must be thin.

No checkered suits please. In the old days checkered suits caused strobing under the lights. Today they are just distracting.

Unless you are thin, stay away from three-button suits and never button up the top or lower buttons. Also, remember to remove glasses, wallets and pens from your jacket pockets, as they tend to create unattractive bulges.

A short person should not wear wide-patterned clothes. A tall person should not wear anything with too many stripes (up and down).

In most cases, a vertical line is the most flattering for men, and it is wise to avoid horizontals.

A good rule to follow for women's clothing is that the simpler the outfit, the better it will look.

Pastel colours are again preferable for television. Do not clutter your neck with scarves or distracting jewellery.

V-neck style tops are preferable.

Stay away from prints, paisleys and checks.

Chapter 13

Do's

PREPARE FOR THE INTERVIEW

Make sure that you know how long the interview will run on air. This will allow you to formulate longer or shorter answers and to make sure that all the important points are covered.

Know your facts, of course. Be ready with statistics, anecdotes (short ones) and any other facts that can make you an exciting guest. If you need some written figures, take them with you. It can be impressive to show them at the right time.

Mention the name of your company. Public awareness is very important.

BE IN CONTROL

Of course, you are on the show to answer questions. But, as you remember from our earlier chapter, you can change the direction of the interview with ease. A good way of doing this is to paraphrase the question, change it slightly, and then answer your own question with the point you want to make.

HAVE AN AGENDA

The interview is a two-way conversation. You have to know what you want to say. Have a lead and examples.

BRIDGE

Answer a negative question briefly and move on to something positive and elaborate on it. To prepare for this, write down the uncomfortable things people could ask you about. Also write down the most positive things you want to talk about and practice ways to get from a negative to a positive position.

ASK QUESTIONS

A very effective way to get out of an uncomfortable situation is to answer a question with a question.

Ask the interviewer what he or she thinks of the topic and politely insist that you are interested in their opinion.

"NO COMMENT" AND "I DON'T KNOW"

It is all right to say "*no comment*" but you must qualify it: "*I would very much like to answer that question, but I am in no position to do so today. At a later date, when I have the answer, I will be happy to speak to you.*"

If you don't know, say so, but say why you don't know. Remember, no comment is *NEWS*. A nice explanation is an *answer*.

Don'ts

Don't lie

Don't be defensive

Don't hesitate to point out that a question is phrased improperly or is incorrect. Fight off questionable statistics. Have your own ready;"*the facts are ...*"

Don't answer a hypothetical question. Say "*The real situation is ...*"

Don't stand still for loaded prefaces. Interrupt. Say it is wrong. You can't afford to have the interviewer brainwash the audience before they hear from you.

Don't be too serious. Come across as human. Put things in the right perspective.

Don't use jargon, abbreviations and complicated language.

Don't repeat negatives.

Don't lose your temper.

Media Interview Workshops

As is with presentation skills, the best way to learn to do successful media interviews is through practice and simulated workshops. There are many different workshops available, one-on-one coaching, small group workshops with video and large group presentations. Here is an example of a Gabor Group media training workshop:

FULL-DAY WORKSHOP

Length:	9:00 a.m. – 5:00 p.m.
Trainers:	Two
Participants:	Four
9:00 – 10:15	Introduction. Discussion of experience with the media. Goals and concerns. Discussion of the media, role of reporters, editors, interviewers, producers. Differences and similarities between the different media. Preparing for media interviews. How to take control. How to get communications messages across. Preparing the interview agenda.
10:15 – 12:00	Simulated media interview #1. The soft talk-show interview. Each interview is recorded, then played back for discussion with focus on control and ability to get key messages across.
12:00 – 1:00	Lunch
1:00 – 2:45	Simulated media interview #2 A tougher more confrontational approach. Radio, print or television. Recorded for playback and discussion.
2:45 – 4:00	The news clip. The 30-second sound bite.
4:00 – 4:30	Social Media.
4:30 – 5:00	Discussion, Q&A and wrap up. Print materials distributed.

I HOPE YOU FOUND THIS HANDBOOK USEFUL.

Remember

Naturals are made as well as born

and

Prepare, Rehearse, Enjoy

GOOD LUCK

Made in United States
North Haven, CT
12 February 2022